NEW ZEALAND LANDSCAPES

NEW ZEALAND LANDSCAPES

PHOTOGRAPHS BY ANDRIS APSE
INTRODUCTION BY ANDY DENNIS

CRAIG
POTTON
PUBLISHING

DEDICATION

To the memory of my mother Kamilla

— Acknowledgements —

There are many people whose generous assistance over the last 20 years has enabled me to collect thousands of images

throughout New Zealand and indeed in many remote corners of the world.

This book features approximately 100 of these images. Many of the photographs would have been difficult if not impossible to

achieve without the generous assistance of the following people: Alan Bond, Richard Hayes, Tim Innes, Lou Sanson, Dave Saxton,

Jeff Shanks, Ken Tustin and Simon Williamson.

Mr Bond, before your head begins to swell out of proportion to your position, the placement of your name in the above list is purely alphabetical.

Published by Craig Potton Publishing,
98 Vickerman Street, PO Box 555,
Nelson, New Zealand

Photography: Andris Apse
Introduction: Andy Dennis
Editing and captions: David Chowdhury
Design: Jo Williams Design
Publishing Coordinator: Robbie Burton
Printed in Hong Kong by Everbest Printing Co Ltd

First published 1994
Reprinted 1995, 1996, 1997, 1998

ISBN 0 908802 23 4

Photograph previous page: Lake Hawea, Central Otago

CONTENTS

Upper Bowen Falls, Milford Sound.

INTRODUCTION

I don't remember exactly when it was that I first became aware of a photographer called Andris Apse, perhaps because he is a modest and private man and seemingly not given to proclaiming his talents with an excessive amount of song and dance. It might have been in the glossy tourist publications which regularly featured his work during the 1980s, or in one of those omnibus volumes about New Zealand landscapes that also emerged during those same years, like Kenneth Cumberland's "Landmarks" or Reader's Digest's "Wild New Zealand". At all events, by the beginning of the 1990s I had begun soliciting a few photographs from him each year for a range of wild places calendars I was involved in helping to produce. And each time a bundle of Apse transparencies arrived in our Nelson office I felt a real hankering for the wild country from which his images were drawn. I felt too that the impact of these photographs was very much enhanced by the way he consistently seemed able to capture beautiful or dramatic light. And there was clearly also something unusually satisfying about lingering over images of landscapes that had been composed in panoramic format. As far as I was aware Andris was one of very few landscape photographers in New Zealand who were then working principally in this extended format, and it seemed to me to provide him with a distinct advantage over others working in this same field.

Photography first became a major component of Andris' destiny in 1963, when the then young Forest Service woodsman landed himself a job with the Forest and Range Experiment Station in Rangiora near Christchurch. Here he began a phase of his life that took him on surveys to the vast and remote wilderness of Fiordland and brought him into regular contact with the renowned Forest Service photographer John Johns. On these survey trips to Fiordland, and to the North Island's Kaweka Ranges, he quickly fell in love with New Zealand's unspoiled natural wilderness, which seemed to him an infinitely preferable environment to production forests planted in straight rows. Fiordland especially he found wonderfully wild and empty and was totally overwhelmed by its beauty and scenic grandeur. He immediately found himself wishing he had some means of recording these magnificent vistas - and more or less decided there and then to try and become a photographer. That this was not an impossible dream was evident to him in the work of John Johns, whose black and white photographs of Fiordland reminded him of aspects of Chinese painting in the way that they seemed at times to reach beyond mere physical portrayal of forests, fiords and mountains towards some deeper awareness of the region's intrinsic character. Accordingly, Andris was soon the proud owner of the first of his many cameras (in this case an Agfa "Clack") which over the next few years he carried with him everywhere, gradually learning that there was a great deal more to the art of landscape photography than simply pointing his camera at some inspiring piece of scenery and pressing the shutter button!

This pioneer period in Andris' life came to an end in 1970 when Rangiora chemist Neil Harrison helped him to buy a local photographic business that by chance had come up for sale. Thus he was able to embark on a career as a professional photographer, albeit one that was dominated in the early years not by wilderness landscapes but by a more mundane diet of portrait, passport and wedding photography. Trips to the wilds during these years were few and far between, and instead Andris devoted his energies to building up the business and advancing his knowledge of the properties of light and lenses and film. The bid for freedom from this routine photographic fare was eventually made in 1978 when he plucked up the courage to purchase a Linhof Technorama camera, capable of producing wide format "panoramic" transparencies 6cm in depth by 17cm in length. This was the only camera of its type in New Zealand at the time and its $5000 price tag was a huge sum for a small-town photographer to contemplate paying for an essential item of photographic equipment, let alone a device as novel (and as radical) as this. But somehow Andris managed to convince the bank that he was the person fated to become its new owner, a decision which, in the event, neither had subsequent cause to regret. Indeed, immediately he began exploring its exciting innovative possibilities, Andris realised that here at last was a camera that was perfectly suited both to his own photographic inclinations and to the dimensions of the kind of landscapes that had first enticed him into photog-

Wandering albatross, Adams Island, Auckland Islands.

raphy, and to which he had always remained determined to devote more time.

The door leading back to landscape work that was pushed ajar by the purchase of the panoramic camera was finally flung wide open in the early 1980s when Andris returned from a wonderful year's travelling through Chile with his young family and decided that the moment had finally come to devote himself full time to photographing landscapes. If at that time he could have written his own job description it would probably have been as a freelance photographer for National Geographic magazine, maintaining a New Zealand base, but regularly out on assignment in other parts of the world. Today, however, he no longer dreams this dream, and although he now sees himself as more ambitious photographically than he was a decade ago, he feels no desperate need to venture beyond New Zealand to satisfy these ambitions. Indeed, he would be more than content to spend the next 20 years confined to Fiordland, and would regard his labours as amply rewarded if he was able to turn out one good landscape photograph a week from its vast store of mountains, valleys, fiords, forests, lakes, rivers and wilderness coastline.

For 150 years or more, writers, painters and photographers have been drawing attention to the fact that New Zealand as a whole contains a variety of landscapes and scenery unmatched anywhere else in the world, which is exceptional within such a compact area. In this small country have been gathered together numerous graphic examples of the great earth-shaping processes of tectonic upheaval, volcanic mayhem and massive glaciation. Coupled with factors like 80 million years of isolation from other large land areas and a frequent occurrence of climatic extremes, these processes have resulted in the highest mountains in Australasia, the most accessible glaciers in the world's temperate regions, a huge and wonderfully diverse expanse of coastline (regularly stated as being in excess of 10,000km), large tracts of virgin rainforest, stark areas of semi-arid terrain, and a liberal sprinkling of highly individual flourishes in things like intriguing areas of karst (or limestone) landscapes and dazzling examples of geothermal creativity. Here too dramatic contrasts abound, often in close proximity - dry eastern areas and a vastly wetter west; gentle plains terminating in abrupt mountain ranges; a subtropical north and a distinctly temperate south; and large areas of essentially untouched natural wilderness giving way, often quite abruptly, to settled landscapes from which all traces of former wildness have often been erased. Qualities like these - and this is by no means a comprehensive catalogue - go some way towards explaining how it is that a photographer of Andris' talents and ambition is able to find everything he needs to satisfy his artistic inclinations without feeling the necessity of travelling to distant lands.

There are, in my experience, five principal factors that determine the outcome of any attempt at photographing landscape. These are: the level of technical understanding and skill in the use of cameras, lenses, filters and film; an eye for both subject matter and for composition; an inspirational feeling for light; a reservoir of patience (and the deeper the better); and, inevitably, some element of luck. With the exception of the last - which, unlike the others, is not wholly in the hands of the photographer - each of these finds ample testimony in the sample of Andris' work that has been included in this collection. Accordingly they provide a convenient framework for taking a closer look at a few of these photographs, and through them, at the landscapes Andris prefers to photograph, and at the way he goes about recording them on film.

In the course of our conversations about photography I asked Andris at one point whether he ever felt confident that he had secured the kind of image he wanted at the moment the shutter was released, or whether, like most of us, he waits with some misgivings until the film arrives back from the processing laboratory. Without the slightest suggestion of arrogance he replied that he now always knew, even before the shutter was released, what the outcome would be. So well does he understand his cameras, lenses, filters and films, that if he encounters a landscape that he feels is worth photographing he has no doubts at all about his ability to capture it on film, regardless of the technical problems it may happen to present. His equipment bag usually includes at least five different types of transparency film and a range of seven different filters, and it is a measure of his dedication to familiarising himself with these basic tools of his trade that when experimenting with a new type of film he expects it to take him at least a hundred rolls before he can feel completely confident about that film's performance under the range of conditions to which he is likely to subject it. Because film is able to reproduce the effects of natural light only within a very restricted range of conditions, most of the photographs in this collection have been filtered - and in some cases heavily filtered - but his aim in using filters is rarely merely cosmetic enhancement. Rather, it is an endeavour to reproduce the natural qualities of the atmosphere and light that were present when the photograph was taken. And it seems to me clear confirmation that Andris is a technician of exceptional skill that in most cases - including those photographs that involve difficult lighting situations - the evidence of his use of filters will not usually be apparent to the great majority of those who confront the results.

While Andris is happy enough to take advantage of most modern developments in the manufacture of filters and film, he remains much more of a traditionalist in his choice of cameras. Having at some time in the past experimented with just about every good quality medium-format camera that has been produced and found them wanting - not necessarily because of optical inadequacies, but rather their inability to survive in the kind of conditions he is likely to subject them to - he has now resorted to having his cameras custom-built to suit his own particular needs. Although these unique devices make use of the very best Schneider lenses and other components of similar impeccable credentials, they are, in many respects, the antithesis of the high-tech cameras produced by most modern manufacturers. They have, for example, only manual functions for aperture, shutter speed and focusing. There is no through-the-lens viewing (so Andris is unable to study his landscapes through the lens transmitting images on to his film). And there are no electronic aids or computerised brains. They are, in reality, much more akin to the type of cameras people like Ansel Adams were using half a century ago than to the sophisticated devices employed by most modern

professionals. Which simply means that in order to take a photograph Andris has to be able to carry out each of these critical functions himself - once, that is, he has sorted out the equally critical preliminary decisions about lenses, filters and film.

As well as providing abundant evidence of a high level of technical skill, these photographs also convey, almost invariably, a very satisfying feeling of aesthetic harmony, even when the mood of the landscape - or seascape - is itself far from harmonious. Time and again I have found myself feeling that the arrangement of the various components is wholly appropriate - almost as if Andris has himself been able to stage-manage the construction of the settings to his own specifications. For example, in the winter photograph of the Ahuriri Valley (p.71) I can picture him searching backwards and forwards for hours on a terrace that

Twisted and gnarled remnant rata forest and wind-blasted coastal shrubs on Enderby Island, Auckland Island group.

has provided him with an elevated lookout across the snow-covered valley floor, trying to assemble the intriguing pattern of river meanders and scattered willows into a composition that he feels will do justice to the landscape as he sees it. Again, in the lovely high country study of Lake Onslow on the following pages, painstaking selection of his photographic standpoint and a careful choice of lens has given him a landscape in perfect balance, with gently rolling tussock ridges carrying the viewer through both foreground and background to the cluster of fishing huts on a sunlit promontory in the centre of the picture. Here, too, the pattern of cloud and clear sky balance the arrangement of land and lake water, and a subtle interplay of light and shadow seems wholly in keeping with the overall atmosphere of remoteness and tranquillity.

In both these photographs, as indeed in most others in this book, the compositional qualities are, it seems to me, greatly enhanced by the use of panoramic format. In the case of the former the width of the composition has allowed the full sweep of the river meanders to be included in the foreground without the distancing that a wide-angle lens would have produced, while in the latter one is left with the feeling that nothing has been omitted from the composition that might in some way have furthered the effect. (As a further test of this meticulous attention to composition try cropping either of these photographs, even to a fairly modest degree, and see what you lose as a consequence!) The results can be even more dramatic in the ultra-wide (6x17) compositions, not only in the case of great sweeps of country like at Ben Avon Station (p.82), Lake Leeb and the Haast Range (p.100), or the intricate weave of arms and islands in Dusky Sound (p.17), but also in photographs of more limited physical focus like the sand dunes on Ninety Mile Beach (p.28), the wind-blasted macrocarpa trees near Pahia in Southland (p.60), or the forest interior from Fiordland's Wild Natives Valley (p.44). It is perhaps worth adding in this context that although Andris began his experiments in panoramic photography with a 6x17 camera his present pattern of use tends to favour the "narrower" 6x12 format. Part of the reason for this is undoubtedly the more limited commercial market for ultra-wide transparencies, at least without cropping (which I'm sure he hates to see happen to any of his careful compositions). But I suspect that there are also aesthetic reasons involved in this choice. The 6x12 seems more akin to normal scope of human vision and hence the way we would take in a comfortable slice of the landscape if we had been present to observe the actual scene. It also better suits compositions where the main focus of attention runs vertically through the centre of the photograph, as it does, for example, with the evening serenity of a stunning Mt Aspiring (p.105), or those two superb studies of solitary seabirds against the bleak but dramatically beautiful landscape of subantarctic Adams Island (p.7 and p.117).

Besides making an initial bid for our attention a successful landscape photograph is surely also one that draws us back again and again for closer contemplation, and, perhaps, for further discoveries. The light-house at Katiki Point (p.26), for example, has provided the focus of another beautifully crafted photograph, wrapped in an atmosphere of wind and storm and seeming isolation. But look again. The road shows little evidence of traffic since the last time it was graded. And a cow, alone in a paddock, peers disconsolately across the road to where two others at least have each other for company. Did Andris notice these things, I wonder? Or did he just see a scene that for other reasons (the line of the road and fences; the lighthouse itself; the general atmosphere) felt to him like a good image, albeit one whose components combined to create a powerful sense of loneliness and isolation?

The lighting, of course, makes an enormous contribution to the total effect of photographs like this, and I can't escape the conclusion that even the most perfect arrangement of terrestrial components would fail as a photograph if the operator of the elemental switchboard was in an uncooperative mood. What for me provides the main emotional impact of many of these photographs - and, I think, lifts a considerable number of them from competently crafted images to genuine examples of art - is the quality of the light that has been added to the compositions. Indeed, so struck was I by the dramatic contribution of light on the first occasion I had access to this collection, that I suggested to the publishers that the subtitle "Landscape and Light" should be added to the front cover. Among photographs already mentioned, those of Lake Onslow (p.72), the Southland macrocarpas (p.60), and Mt Aspiring (p.105) are all beautiful examples of landscape and light, as are most of the images chosen to accompany this introduction, especially those from Lake Hawea (p.3) and Adams Island (p.7). In the latter of these it was, I suspect, the solitary young bird and dramatic ramparts of sea cliffs that initially caught my attention. But what brings me back again and again to this particular photograph is the way threatening black clouds hang over the summit of the island, sunlight dances out across much of the sea, and the whole scene in between becomes a pattern of different moods of intimacy and remoteness - or, perhaps, of security and alienation - as the effects of the dramatic lighting interact with the structural elements of the composition. In the case of the ranges beyond Lake Hawea the composition is constructed not around features assembled in the centre of the photograph but of landscape components which are horizontally arranged, and in perfect harmony with this structural pattern. The lighting on both land and sky occurs in a series of dramatic horizontal bands of sunlight and shadow.

I must admit that I find it very much easier to say of these photographs simply that they are "beautifully lit" or "dramatically lit" rather than to try and explain in words what is partly (and perhaps at times wholly) an intuitive emotional response. The first three photographs mentioned in the preceding paragraph all seem to me to be beautifully lit, as are many of the rural landscapes (both in the intensity of the greens and the patterns of light and shadow), and virtually all of the photographs of indigenous forest, including those of more sombre connotation, like the beech forest bordering the tumbling stream at the head of George Sound (p.36 and p.47). In other contexts too, sombre lighting is able to provide a kind of melancholic beauty that is often absent from popular photographic books on "Beautiful New Zealand", examples of which are the

Hoopers Inlet and Allans Beach, Otago Peninsula.

lovely atmospheric study of Penguin Bay on Otago Peninsula (p.29), or the wonderfully Stygian sea-scape (yes, I know, the Styx was a river) of crepuscular Cape Reinga (p.18).

Dramatic lighting, in contrast, tends to be patchy rather than pervasive (though this is not always the case), and includes those photographs whose effects have been at least partially manufactured by the photographer, either by creative use of filters or by techniques like deliberately shooting against the sun. Examples of the latter include images like the golden dawn over Nugget Point (p.15), or the graphic highlighting of braided channels in the high country sections of the Rakaia River (p.80). I must confess, however, that while I remain intrigued by these effects my clear personal preference is for drama generated by lighting that comes unmanipulated from the elements, as it does to such wonderful effect on the ranges and clouds near Lake Hawea (p.87), the farmland near Kyeburn (p.56), or the mystic atmosphere of the snowfields at the head of the Fox Glacier (p.92). In the last of these, patches of dramatic light flood down upon an otherwise dark Fox névé during a brief interlude of elemental cooperation in what was otherwise a week of relentless storms - an emphatic reminder, if indeed we need one, that in landscape photography lighting is very much a gift from the gods, and one that they do not always appear to dispense in just proportion to those who deserve it most.

A little over a year ago I got up daily in the pre-dawn darkness to set up my camera and tripod overlooking the beautiful beach at Sealers' Bay on Codfish Island and waited for a glorious dawn to erupt over the Ruggedy Mountains on nearby mainland Stewart Island. Not an entirely original undertaking, I hasten to add, but rather an attempt to emulate, and perhaps even outdo, the results of a friend's earlier dawn vigils from the same location at much the same time of year. At times the omens seemed to be highly favourable as brooding clouds gathered over the Ruggedy summits while still leaving a band of clear sky on the eastern horizon, conditions tailor-made, or so it seemed, for a dazzling southern sunrise. But despite two weeks of patient perseverance dawn never really managed to happen in the way that I had hoped that it might, and my photographic spoils were accordingly never more than modest.

There is, of course, a rich harvest of other sorts to be gleaned from being up before dawn in wild country despite the lack of cooperation from the elements in achieving photographic objectives, but it is unusual for me - a traveller by nature rather than a watcher - to exhibit the degree of patience that Codfish Island prompted. In Andris' case however, it is the way he prefers to work, whenever he can find the time and space to do so. For example, each year in the spring or early summer he makes a six week expedition to one of a scattering of favourite haunts on the remote Fiordland coast. He makes these trips, quite often alone, with his cameras, supplies and a small aluminium dinghy. He sets up a base camp and begins his patient work, searching for, and then waiting for, that falling together of factors that will result in not just a good photograph, but an exceptional one. Again and again he returns to the same carefully selected locations. And, from time to time, this solitude of forest and sea and mountain and tumbling waters yields him the kind of bounty he is seeking. With photographs like the brooding beech forest and swollen torrent near the head of George Sound (p.13 and p.36). Or the almost mystic serenity of still waters, sunlit islands and mist-veiled forested hillsides of the cover photograph.

I think it must be self-evident that folk who tend to move through country rather than linger for a time in the same place must rely rather more heavily on luck in encountering the concurrence of landscape and light that can result in a good photograph than a patient and meticulous practitioner like Andris. But even Andris sometimes draws a blank. For example, despite numerous carefully timed visits to Lake Matheson he has yet to come home with the kind of photograph that satisfies his own exacting standards. The composition presents few problems - indeed the classic view from the western end of the lake is ideally suited to the wide (or even extra-wide) format. The technical skill is certainly not in question. And his planning will, I am certain, have given careful attention to such matters as the season, the time of day, and the content of the latest weather forecasts. But somehow those crucial elemental ingredients of light and mood have never quite managed to cooperate with Andris in the way he has wanted in respect of this classic West Coast panorama of lake and forest and mountains and sky. In much the same vein, for a week or ten days immediately prior to my first meeting with him he was away on another journey to the subantarctic Auckland Islands. He had eagerly accepted the opportunity to join a naval expedition to these far-flung outliers of New Zealand that are said, by those who have been there, to be wonderful for plants and seabirds and marine mammals but awful for people. Except, I suspect, for people like Andris, who find in their uncompromised wildness, intense low-angled light, and violent shifts in weather and mood, an unusually fertile environment for artistic landscape photography. But, as luck would have it on this particular voyage, the elements prevented access to the shore at the times which would have yielded the results he wanted, and thus Andris was denied a rare opportunity to add to his collection of subantarctic landscape photographs.

Besides reminding us that there will always be some element of landscape photography that remains beyond the control of even the most painstaking practitioner, these two episodes provide further clear evidence of the lengths to which Andris is prepared to go in pursuit of his photographic objectives. In fact, in an odd sort of way that I'm not sure I can fully explain, they seem somehow to reinforce my conviction that the photographs assembled here ultimately owe far more to the kind of qualities I have attempted to describe than they do to any mere matter of chance - that is, to the pains Andris has taken to perfect his craft; to the care he invests over the way he fills his frame; to the appreciation he very clearly has of the contribution made by light; and to the huge amount of patience he is obviously prepared to invest in order to get photographs of a standard that he feels does justice both to the landscapes and to his own artistic goals. Indeed, the only photograph in this book that is the outcome of a chance encounter rather than of careful planning and patient execution is that of the onset of a nor'west storm over the Hawdon Valley (p.79) - reminiscent of Petrus van der Velden's paintings of the Otira Gorge - fortuitously taken from the roadside during a journey across Arthur's Pass.

These reflections on patience and luck seem to me an appropriate point to end these introductory remarks and allow the photographs some space to speak for themselves. Perhaps as others work through them they too will be reminded of the years of patience required to assemble a collection as memorable as this, and of how lucky we are that people exist who are prepared to devote their lives to enabling the rest of us to see, by the simple act of opening a book, what is beautiful and moving about landscapes and light.

Andy Dennis

Alice Falls at the top of George Sound, Fiordland National Park.

THE COASTLINE

Gathering cloudbank over Portobello, Otago Peninsula, at sunset.

Nugget Point, eroded rock stacks and cliffs at sunrise, Catlins Coast, South Otago.

FACING PAGE: Mitre Peak, Milford Sound.

ABOVE: Glacier shaped islands and headlands at the entrance to Dusky Sound, Fiordland National Park.

OVERLEAF: Cape Reinga, the northernmost point of the New Zealand mainland, at dusk.

Facing Page: Breaksea Sound, Fiordland National Park.

Above: Placid seas at sunrise looking north toward Kaikoura Peninsula from the Kahutara River mouth.

[20]

LEFT: Castlepoint, Wairarapa Coast.

ABOVE: Limestone/sedimentary bluffs below Castlepoint Lighthouse.

OVERLEAF: Morning cloud disperses from Milford Sound's buttresses and Mitre Peak after a southwesterly storm.

Katiki Point lighthouse near Moeraki, Otago, looking south.

Ocean swells erupt spectacularly through blowholes at Punakaiki in North Westland's Paparoa National Park.

Tidal sand patterns near Pakawau, Golden Bay.

RIGHT: Storm driven surf surges onto Penguin Beach on the Otago Peninsula.

Cape Maria Van Dieman, North Cape, Northland.

South Westland coast from Knights Point near Haast.

Rain showers sweep across Chalky Inlet in the south west of Fiordland National Park.

Sand dunes, Ninety Mile Beach, Northland.

OVERLEAF: Salmon fishing on the Waimakariri River mouth, Canterbury.

LOWLAND WILDERNESS

Alice Falls, George Sound, Fiordland National Park.

Forest trunks and tree ferns, Breaksea Sound, Fiordland National Park.

Korokoro Falls, Urewera National Park.

Ferns and broadleaved shrubs and trees in streamway, Kaipo Valley, Fiordland National Park.

Sunset over the Fraser Peaks range and Port Pegasus, Stewart Island.

RIGHT: A tributary to Wild Natives River in Bligh Sound, Fiordland National Park.

Styx River chasm, near Lake Kaniere, Westland.

A grove of nikau palms at Kahurangi Point on the west coast of Kahurangi National Park, northwest Nelson.

OVERLEAF: Moss draped ribbonwood forest and blechnum ferns at Kiwi Lake, Wild Natives Valley, Fiordland National Park.

Beech forest interior in the Freeman Burn above North Arm of Lake Manapouri, Fiordland National Park.

Small forest waterfall at the head of George Sound, Fiordland.

PASTORAL LAND

Stooked oats on a North Canterbury farm.

Hereford cattle grazing farmland beneath the Southern Alps near Fox Glacier.

Rolling farmland near Balclutha.

RIGHT: Southern Alps, foothills, Canterbury Plains and the Rakaia River.

Otago Harbour (left), Otago Peninsula and Hoopers Inlet, from Peggy's Hill.

Coromandel Harbour and offshore islands from Pukewhakataratara, Coromandel Peninsula.

Last light on nor'west cloud patterns, near Fernside, North Canterbury.

Mudstone hill country farmland near Tahora in the Taumarunui district, King Country.

OVERLEAF: Golden fields and river escarpment near Kyeburn, North Otago.

The barley harvest at 'Woodlands', near Temuka, South Canterbury.

Tolaga Bay farmland, East Cape.

Twisted and wind shorn macrocarpa trees at Pahia on Southland's southern coast.

Sheep flock being herded on undulating downs at 'Woodlands' near Temuka, South Canterbury.

Valley mist rises from the frosted banks and trees of the Clutha River
(these river flats have since been flooded by Lake Dunstan which has formed behind the Clyde Dam).

Autumn poplars and willows at Macetown, Central Otago.

OVERLEAF: Grasslands near Palmerston North.

Hill country south of the Waitaki Valley and the Waitaki River floodplain beyond.

Rolling green hills near Cheviot, North Canterbury.

Overleaf: Church, cemetery and barley crop near Taihape, northern Manawatu.

HIGH COUNTRY

Douglas firs in autumn and the Mt Cook massif from the shores of Lake Pukaki.

Upper Ahuriri Valley after mid-winter snowfall, Mackenzie Country.

Sunrise at Lake Onslow, east of Roxburgh in Central Otago.

From Mt John above Lake Tekapo in the Mackenzie Country looking northwest towards the Southern Alps foothills.

Drowned willows in Lake Wanaka.

OVERLEAF: Rain clouds approaching Lake Manapouri from the Fiordland mountains.

Erewhon Station, Taihape, northern Manawatu.

A dust storm in the Hawdon Valley heralds the arrival of a nor'west storm over Arthur's Pass National Park.

The sunlit braids of the Rakaia River flow from the Southern Alps towards the Canterbury Plains.

High country cattle muster on Birchwood Station in the upper Dingle Burn, east of Lake Hawea, Central Otago.

Overleaf: Ben Avon Station, upper Ahuriri Valley.

Limestone tors and sheep during winter feedout at Castle Hill, mid-Canterbury high country.

Musterers on a high ridge in the upper Dingle Burn, Otago.

Musterer and dogs on Dalrachney Station, near Lindis Pass, Otago.

West over Lake Hawea towards Mt Aspiring (obscured) and peaks of Mt Aspiring National Park.

Overleaf: Lake Wanaka and the Southern Alps from Roys Peak.

MOUNTAINS

The Torlesse Range from Castle Hill Village, Canterbury.

Climbers on Pioneer Ridge, upper Fox Glacier, Westland National Park.

OVERLEAF: Skiers on the Fox Glacier, Westland National Park.

Waiwhakaiho River and Mt Egmont/Taranaki, Egmont National Park.

Mt Tasman, Mt Cook and Mt Sefton from the southwest.

OVERLEAF: Stormbound Southern Alps from the head of Lake Tekapo looking north up the Godley Valley.

A "hogsback" storm cloud enshrouds Mt Cook at sunset. From the Hooker Valley, Mt Cook National Park.

Mt Tasman (centre) and Mt Cook, from a ridge high above the Fox Glacier in Westland National Park.

OVERLEAF: Lake Leeb above the Arawata Valley looking east to the Haast Range, South Westland.

Nor'west arch over Lake Pukaki, looking north towards Mt Cook.

Lake Roe in the Merrie Mountains near the head of the Hauroko Burn, southern Fiordland National Park.

Cascade below Lake Freeman in the upper Freeman Burn above Lake Manapouri's
North Arm, Fiordland National Park.
RIGHT: Mt Aspiring and the Bonar Glacier from the southwest.
Mt Cook on left distant horizon.

The western edge of Fiordland National Park from above Catseye Bay, looking south.

Hump Ridge tarn, south of Lake Hauroko, southern Fiordland National Park.

Sunrise over End Peak and Treble Cone, near Lake Wanaka, Central Otago.

Mt Ngauruhoe at sunset, Tongariro National Park.

ISLANDS

Steam and sulphur vapour from the White Island volcano, Bay of Plenty.

Sulphur deposits and steaming fumaroles in the White Island crater.

Volcanic cliffs on the southern edge of subantarctic Adams Island in the Auckland Islands group, 600km south of mainland New Zealand.

Embrasure Point and wind-blasted waterfall, Adams Island, Auckland Islands group.

Southern rata trunks, Auckland Island.

Rugged Point on the northwest corner of Stewart Island.

Erect crested penguin colony and rock stack, Antipodes Island, 1000km southeast of New Zealand.

Sooty albatross nesting amongst megaherbs on a rock outcrop above Fly Harbour, Adams Island, Auckland Islands.

Mason Bay dunelands, Stewart Island.

Ruggedy Mountains from Waituna Beach, northwest Stewart Island.

Buller's mollymawks circling above rock stacks on Solander Island, northwest of Stewart Island.